What is Money?

Ben Hubbard
and Beatriz Castro

CRABTREE
PUBLISHING COMPANY
WWW.CRABTREEBOOKS.COM

CRABTREE
PUBLISHING COMPANY
WWW.CRABTREEBOOKS.COM

Author: Ben Hubbard

Editorial director: Kathy Middleton

Editors: Julia Bird

Proofreader: Ellen Rodger

Illustrator: Beatriz Castro

Prepress technician: Ken Wright

Print coordinator: Katherine Berti

Every attempt has been made to clear copyright. Should there be any inadvertent omission please apply to the publisher for rectification.

The website addresses (URLs) included in this book were valid at the time of going to press. However, it is possible that contents or addresses may have changed since the publication of this book. No responsibility for any such changes can be accepted by either the author or the Publisher.

Library and Archives Canada Cataloguing in Publication

Title: What is money? / Ben Hubbard and [illustrated by] Beatriz Castro.
Names: Hubbard, Ben, 1973- author. | Castro, Beatriz (Castro Arbaizar), illustrator.
Description: Series statement: All about money | Previously published: London: Franklin Watts, 2019. | Includes index.
Identifiers: Canadiana (print) 20190195371 | Canadiana (ebook) 2019019538X | ISBN 9780778773818 (hardcover) | ISBN 9780778773856 (softcover) | ISBN 9781427125002 (HTML)
Subjects: LCSH: Finance, Personal—Juvenile literature. | LCSH: Money—Juvenile literature.
Classification: LCC HG179 .H834 2020 | DDC j332.024—dc23

Library of Congress Cataloging-in-Publication Data

Names: Hubbard, Ben, 1973- author. | Castro, Beatriz (Castro Arbaizar), illustrator.
Title: What is money? / Ben Hubbard and ; Beatriz Castro.
Description: New York, New York : Crabtree Publishing Company, [2019] | Series: All about money | Includes index.
Identifiers: LCCN 2019043488 (print) | LCCN 2019043489 (ebook) | ISBN 9780778773818 (hardcover) | ISBN 9780778773856 (paperback) | ISBN 9781427125002 (ebook)
Subjects: LCSH: Money--Juvenile literature.
Classification: LCC HG221.5 .H83 2019 (print) | LCC HG221.5 (ebook) | DDC 332.4--dc23
LC record available at https://lccn.loc.gov/2019043488
LC ebook record available at https://lccn.loc.gov/2019043489

Crabtree Publishing Company

www.crabtreebooks.com   1–800–387–7650
Published by Crabtree Publishing Company in 2020

Printed in the U.S.A./012020/CG20191115

Published in Canada
Crabtree Publishing
616 Welland Ave.
St. Catharines, Ontario
L2M 5V6

Published in the United States
Crabtree Publishing
PMB 59051
350 Fifth Avenue, 59th Floor
New York, New York 10118

What is Money?

This book is all about money. Why is money important? You can't eat or drink it, but most of us need money to survive. We use money to pay for nearly everything we need or want, including clothing, electricity, food, and water. It is hard to imagine a world without money.

Some people say money makes the world go around.

When we have some money, we have to make choices.
What should we do with our money? We can:

Save it

Spend it

Share it

Or, make more money!

In this book, Leo asks, "What is money?"
Keep reading to find out!

Leo is nearly seven. But he can't ever remember seeing any money in his house. This is because his dad does the supermarket shopping **online**, his mom buys clothes with her **credit card**, and his sister pays for things using her phone.

They say they are buying things—but where is the money hidden?

Most people keep their money safe in a bank. They use cards, phones, and online banking to spend it.

7

9

On the way to school, Leo and his dad look at cars for sale. The most expensive cars are new and shiny, but there are cheaper, **used** cars, too. Leo spots a car he likes.

At school, Leo feels confused. He has some money, but he can't afford a sports car. Money comes with so many rules! At lunchtime, Leo and his friends simply **trade** their food with each other. Isn't trading things better than buying them?

In class, Leo's teacher explains the history of bartering. Before money was invented, everyone used to barter. This means they would swap something they had for something someone else had.

Thousands of years ago, bartering was the only way to get the things you needed.

Will you take this basket of fish for your chicken?

I love fish. It's a deal.

Leo's teacher says money was invented to replace bartering. The first money was not paper bills and coins. Instead, people used grain, iron tools, and seashells as money. Any object could act as money, as long as everyone agreed on what it was worth.

In ancient Egypt, grain was valuable. It was used as money. Grain was kept safe in **granaries**, which are like banks for grain.

Thank you for your deposit of 200 bowls of grain.

I'll be back tomorrow to withdraw 20 bowls. I need it to pay for a cruise on the Nile.

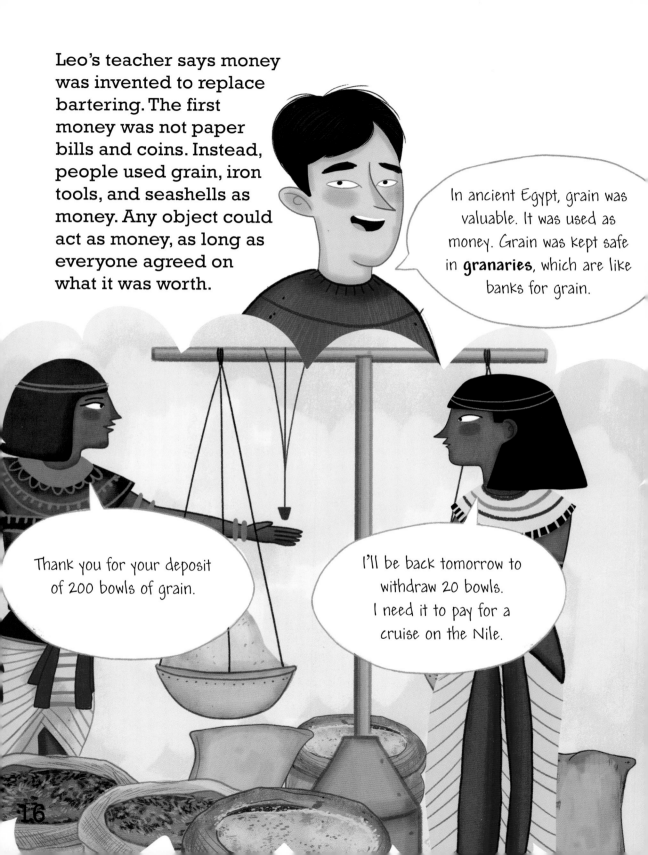

16

17

In the 800s CE, China was the first country to use paper money. The Italian explorer Marco Polo later brought the idea to Europe.

Paper money was first used in Europe in the 1600s. In England, some people gave their gold to **goldsmiths** to keep it safe for them in strong boxes, called safes. The goldsmiths would give them a note saying how much gold they had stored there. These banknotes became the paper money, or bills, we use today.

After school, Leo goes to the bank with his mom. At the bank, Leo asks to trade his ten-dollar bill for ten gold pieces. But the bank manager says banknotes don't stand for gold anymore.

Currencies around the world

Your ten-dollar bill might not be the same value as gold, but it could be used to buy a tiny amount of gold. Or you could buy some money from a different country.

Every country has their own money, called **currency**. When people go on vacation to another country, they buy some of that country's currency. They use it to buy things when they get there.

 **£**

United Kingdom: Pound Sterling

 **$**

United States of America: United States Dollar

 €

Eurozone: European Euro

 **¥**

China: Chinese Yuan

 ₽

Russia: Russian Ruble

 **₹**

India: Indian Rupee

 **R$**

Brazil: Brazilian Real

 $

Canada: Canadian Dollar

Rp

Indonesia: Indonesian Rupiah

 **$**

Australia: Australian Dollar

The bank manager tells Leo that he could use his money to open a bank account with a parent. Then Leo won't have to carry his money around with him. Instead, the bank will keep it safe until he spends it.

You can use this bankbook to keep track of the money you put in and take out of the bank.

Can I have a **debit card**, too?

If your mom allows it, you can also withdraw money using a debit card at an ATM, or automated teller machine.

You can spend money:

Online

On the phone

By debit card

As cash

At home, Leo shows his dad his bankbook.
They go onto his online account together.

Leo is feeling very grown-up now that he has a bank account. He could save his money and watch it grow over time—or he could spend it! When he is out with his mom, Leo sees a lot of things he'd like to buy.

Look at that, Mom. I need that model car!

But you don't really need it, Leo. You already have everything you need: a home and a loving family.

Leo didn't realize that having some money came with so many choices. But he has learned a lot, too. With his new knowledge, he uses his money in several different ways:

Leo saves some money

I'm saving $5 and will use the allowance I get from my parents every week to save even more.

29

QUIZ

Now that you've reached the end of the book, how much do you think you've learned about saving money? Take this test to find out.

1

Where do most people keep their money?

- **a** Buried in the backyard
- **b** In a closet
- **c** In a bank

2

What do people do when they barter?

- **a** Swap things
- **b** Eat things
- **c** Drink things

3

What were the first coins made from?

- **a** Grain
- **b** Bowls
- **c** Electrum

4

Who introduced paper money to Europe?

- **a** Christopher Columbus
- **b** Marco Polo
- **c** Neil Armstrong

5

What is another name for a country's money?

- **a** Currency
- **b** Murrency
- **c** Burrency

Answers
1.c, 2.a, 3.c, 4.b, 5.a

Money words

debit card
A plastic card from a bank that is used at an ATM to withdraw cash or at a store to pay for something

credit card
A plastic card from a bank or a company, used to pay for a product or service. The product or service can then be paid for in full at a later date.

currency
The money system used by a country

goldsmith
Someone who makes gold objects. In the past, goldsmiths also used to act as bankers.

granaries
Places where grain is stored

online
On the Internet

trade
To give something in exchange for another thing

used
When something, such as a bike or some clothing, is not new and has been owned by someone else before

Money facts

There's always more to learn about money.
Check out these facts!

- Paper money is printed onto giant rolls and then cut into the rectangular pieces we carry in our wallets.

- The word bank comes from the old Italian word *banca*, which means bench.

- Rare coins can be sold for large amounts. A U.S. coin made in 1794 is now worth over $10 million dollars!

- Dishonest people used to shave the edge of early gold and silver coins, which was called "clipping." They melted the shavings down to make a new bar of metal, or even new coins. Coins now have an edge with ridges. It would be easy to spot if the ridges were shaved off a coin.

- Most of the U.S. government's gold is stored in a bomb-proof shelter called Fort Knox.